WHEN THE
BOTTOM LINE MATTERS

A Journey through Financial Crises

WHEN THE BOTTOM LINE MATTERS
A JOURNEY THROUGH FINANCIAL CRISES

Copyright © 2009 Dave Keesling

Published by
Dave Keesling Productions
621 Woodland West Drive
Woodland Park, CO 80863

Scripture quotations, unless otherwise marked, are taken from the *New American Standard Bible*®, (Copyright © 1960, 1962, 1963, 1968, 1971, 1972, 1973, (1975, 1977, 1995 byThe Lockman Foundation. Used by permission. (http://www.Lockman.org)

Scripture quotations marked (NIV) are taken from the *Holy Bible, New International Version*®. NIV®. Copyright© 1973, 1978, 1984 by International Bible Society. Used by permission of Zondervan. All rights reserved.

Editorial Consultant
Stephanie Terry, Woodbridge, VA

Cover Design by
ABC Design: Dave Wilson

Interior Design by
The Typecrafter: Wayne Muirheid

ISBN: 978-0-9767161-6-7

Printed in the United States of America

First Edition 2009

10 9 8 7 6 5 4 3 2 1

CONTENTS

INTRODUCTION DAY 5

DAY   1:   VOLUNTEERING FOR DEATH 10

DAY   2:   MOSTLY DEAD 12

DAY   3:   PENALTY BOX 14

DAY   4:   PLUNDERING THE ENEMY 16

DAY   5:   A USEFUL TEST 18

DAY   6:   AMBLE PAST THE CEMETERY 20

DAY   7:   COMPLETE WETNESS 22

DAY   8:   CONFUSING ROLES 24

DAY   9:   FLESHLY NAVIGATION 26

DAY 10:   KNOWING HIS TIMING 28

DAY 11:   PERFECT TRUST 30

DAY 12:   SHORTCOMINGS OF LOINCLOTHS 32

DAY 13:   STAR PEGS AND ROUND HOLES 34

DAY 14:   STEEPED IN FAITH'S TRADITIONS 36

DAY 15:   TIMING IS THE HARD PART 38

DAY 16:   WHICH BURDEN SHALL IT BE 40

DAY 17:   EARLY HIRES 42

DAY 18:   ELEVATOR MANNERS 44

DAY 19:   AFRICAN FIELD HAND 46

DAY 20:   CHASING HER TAIL 48

DAY 21:   IDOLS AT RISK 50

DAY 22:   FROM OOZE TO YOU 52

DAY 23:   BUYER'S REMORSE 54

DAY 24:   COUNTRY BOYS' BLING 56

DAY 25:   MILKWEED AND COCKLEBURS 58

DAY 26:   THE DEEP 60

DAY 27:   SEEING PAST THE SMOKE 49

DAY 28:   LIVING WITH PRICKS AND THORNS 64

DAY 29:   STONES MUST FALL 51

DAY 30:   ENTERING THE LAND 68

DAY 31:   JUST STUFF 70

DAY 32:   SAND CASTLES 72

DAY 33: RECEIVING A DOUBLE PORTION 74
DAY 34: GRACE FOR FULNESS 76
DAY 35: WHEELBARROWS AND TANKERS................................78
DAY 36: TRAIN WRECK..80
DAY 37: COOKIE-JAR GIVING 82
DAY 38: HOGWASH...84
DAY 39: JOANNA'S CROWN 86
DAY 40: ORNAN'S GENEROSITY 88
AFTERWORD 91

INTRODUCTION
You shall have no other gods before Me.
EXODUS 20:3

These words of God have thundered through the ages. Arbitrary, inflexible, threatening words, they also speak of a God whose love for us is so great that He establishes boundaries of the heart in order to protect us. His words speak volumes about a God who says what He means and who is frustratingly unchanging regardless of outward circumstances.

The finger of God had burnished these words into stone tablets Moses would twice carry into the Israelite camp . . . a camp first known for its drunken orgy of wild, misdirected worship, but subsequently one that was appropriately subdued following the punishment meted out by a God who, absent Moses' pleas, would have killed them all.[1]

God's people had sinned all right. No evidence of reigning righteousness could be found as Moses lingered in God's presence on the mountain. As first days then weeks passed without confirmation of Moses' survival, fear grasped the hearts of, apparently, the entire nation. Not even Aaron was spared from cascading uncertainty as everything they had trusted in seemed to have crumbled around them.[3]

What exactly was their sin? Was it simply the building of a golden calf? No, of course not. Their sin was certainly manifest in the calf and in their raising of it to a place of worship. But their sin went much deeper than that. It sprang from hearts weakened by fear of their current circumstances, made faint by fear of a future without Moses' leadership; after all, he represented everything they had known of stability and provision at that point in their lives.

Granted, they had never been wholehearted followers of Moses. There had been complaints aplenty about manna and murmuring over the water supply. There had been fear of Pharaoh's army and a frantic feeling of being boxed in as his advance had pressed their backs against a hopelessly unyielding sea.

But ultimately their complaints, like my own, weren't against outward circumstances, as bleak as they often appeared. Nor was Moses their true nemesis. Their real problem was their own fear-filled hearts.

They feared the loss of security. Having once been pulled from Egypt's brick-making mud pits, the only home they had ever known was now irretrievably lost.

They feared for their lives. Pharaoh's pursuit had not been to recapture a lost workforce, but to kill them.

They feared loss of leadership. Moses had ascended Mt. Sinai weeks earlier without so much as a smoke signal of reassurance from the mountain's flank.[3] Their fears convinced them they were abandoned, leaderless, without secure provision for their future. Their stock market had crashed, their retirement savings sundered. So they gave voice to their fears and danced absurdly around an idol of their own making.

It is worth asking: Am I all that different from them? Are we all that different?

The wealthy, once-comfortable Western world finds itself behaving very much like fearful Israelites of old. Financial props have been knocked from under us, seemingly swallowed by the same blazing fire that consumed the golden calf.[4]

Admittedly, most of us have lost far more than our place in Egypt's mud pits. The jobs we fear losing have paid far better, and the houses at risk are much nicer than those of the ancient Israelites. Our carefully planned retirement whose decline now glares at us like dreams darkened by a broken film in the theater is far grander than the one these ancestors thought had been forsaken as they wandered in the desert.

But are we not the same as they? Don't we deal with the same core issues? Who will be there for us when all we have known, all we have trusted in, one day disappears?

Who exactly is our provider anyway? Has our security ever really rested in a fat 401(k) or a beautiful home on a quintessentially tree-lined American street? Somewhere deep within we have known the answer all along, but too often we have hoped to delay our heart's day of reckoning till after our own season of personal harvest had reached its completion. "Then we will trust You, Lord," has too often been a fair summation of our spiritual maturity.

But we must never forget this: it is in testing that He is manifest. As long as we could meet our own needs through too-easy credit or an insular separation from the hurting among us, we have never truly needed Him. We have too often used the world's financial system as our supply, our own storehouse. It is only when we come to the end of ourselves that He is finally able to break through our self-sufficiency to demonstrate afresh how great is His provision in every area of life.

The devotionals in this book are built around this exact theme. They are about thriving spiritually when the bottom line on which our lives have been built seems to have been swallowed up in the financial and political chaos of the age. They are intended to challenge us to generosity that can only come from recognizing that He, not our balance sheet, is our Source.

These lessons are written in devotional form because they are intended to draw us back to the heart of God. They are designed to challenge us to honestly consider whether His salvation is really complete, whether His provision is more than enough. We are called on to decide once and for all whether we can truly rely on Him and Him alone even as everything around us is shaken to its core.

His promise is to never leave us nor forsake us.[5] And He also promises that one day all the trials and stresses of the age will seem to have been but momentary, light affliction. In that day I will discover that if my full trust has been in Him it will have purchased an eternal weight of glory unsurpassed by all the wealth this world could have provided.[6]

Prayer: Father, I come to You now in humility, asking Your forgiveness for ever thinking I could put my trust in any of this world's goods. Strip away anything I have trusted in that is not You, O Lord. Show me the barrenness of my life when things were at their fleshly zenith. Show me how to enter into Your fulness, that Your limitless reservoir of plenty would become mine. I love you, Lord!

1. Ex. 32:6, 9–14
2. Ex. 32:25
3. Ex. 32:1
4. Ex. 32:20
5. Dt. 31:6
6. 2 Cor. 4:17

WHEN THE BOTTOM LINE MATTERS

A Journey through Financial Crises

Day 1

VOLUNTEERING FOR DEATH

I die daily.
1 CORINTHIANS 15:31

Observation: This simple statement comes in the midst of a discourse by Paul on death and resurrection—on the differences between those who have eternal life in Christ and will be given new and imperishable bodies in the resurrection, and those who do not know Christ, but are simply "earthy" (1 Cor.15:48). Paul seemed to be stretching the capacity of human language to find words to express the soaring joy of experiencing the last enemy to be defeated: death. The passage comes to its sweeping, exuberant conclusion with this incredible outburst, much like the concluding phrases of the 1812 Overture or the "Hallelujah Chorus": "Death is swallowed up in victory. O death, where is your victory? O death, where is your sting?" (vv. 54–55).

Application: The grandeur and massive sweep of Paul's words are overpowering, but I am drawn back to his simple statement, "I die daily."

What an odd thing to say in a chapter that celebrates the end of death. And yet, the reality of daily dying to flesh and pride is the key to the door by which I can experience all the rest. This business of laying down my rights, of surrendering control over my time, my money, even my life itself, this is the essential opening of the passageway that leads to eternal life in Christ.

And that process of voluntary surrender and dying, must be done daily; it is never a once-and-for-all kind of thing. My flesh resists, pride screams that it deserves to be supreme, and indeed, as much as I have cultivated pride over the years, I'm not surprised that it constantly tries to exalt itself. Yet God calls me to once again lay down all the supposed good stuff of my life as though it was filthy rags, at the foot of His cross, that everything I bring might be covered by His blood as it pours from His broken body.

I desire better things—things better than life itself: an imperishable body, one raised in power and glory.

Prayer: Make me spiritually discerning Lord—one who has been so changed into the likeness of Jesus that You would prepare for me a place at the table when You host the wedding feast for Your dear Son and His bride.

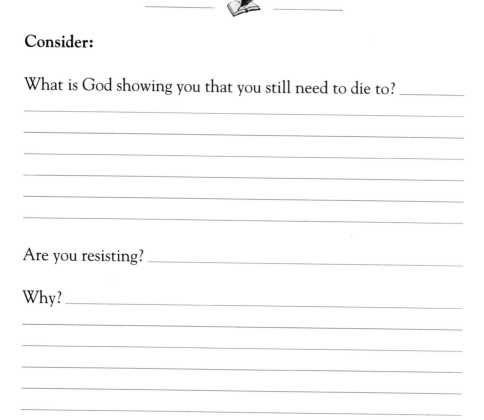

Consider:

What is God showing you that you still need to die to? _____

_____

_____

_____

_____

_____

_____

Are you resisting? _____

Why? _____

_____

_____

_____

_____

_____

Day 2

MOSTLY DEAD

Roam to and fro through the streets of
Jerusalem, and look now and take note. And
seek in her open squares, if you can find a man, if
there is one who does justice, who seeks
truth, then I will pardon her.
JEREMIAH 5:1

Truly, truly I say to you, unless a grain of wheat falls
into the earth and dies, it remains alone; but
if it dies, it bears much fruit. He who loves his life loses
it, and he who hates his life in this
world will keep it to life eternal.
JOHN 12:24–25

Observation: Jeremiah was establishing reasons for the coming judgment. God had commanded that all Jerusalem be searched to seek one righteous person, in which case God would pardon the city from approaching destruction. This passage echoes an earlier challenge to Abraham who had negotiated with God a pardon for another sin-filled city if only enough righteous people could be found. Of course, both Abraham and Jeremiah found that God had correctly assessed the hearts of the people, and destruction followed. But just as this verse is an echo of the past, it also points to a future time and place where the Lord Jesus Christ, in the John passage, describes His own coming death as the model for me to follow in receiving an eternal pardon.

Application: There are important similarities as well as differences between these two passages. In Jeremiah, all wicked people were to pay the price for their sin; none would escape. But in John, only One would die for the sins of many. Jesus Himself, the innocent one, would take my sin upon Himself, and His death would be a gateway to eternal life in Him. John 12:25 calls me to lose my life in order to save it, to hate the life of the world and the flesh and all the striving that daily presses in. As a result, He promises I will enter into His life for eternity.

My problem is this: it is a constant battle to die effectively. Like the wizard in *Princess Bride* who pronounces the corpse only "mostly dead," so it seems that the tug of the world lingers in the background of my soul, always eager to tempt me again into pursuing temporal pleasures rather than pure unity with God. So the struggle continues with battle lines stark, sharp, and without compromise. Sin cannot be only "mostly dead"; it is either all dead or it is not dead at all. Similarly, there is in God's economy no such thing as being "mostly righteous." His call to me is to enter fully into His death, that I might gain His life.

Prayer: Lord Jesus, You have pointed the way. You have told me clearly what must be done to enter into Your life. Search my heart for areas of compromise, Lord. Show me what You see there, that I might make a fresh decision to crucify all that is not of You.

Consider:

If Jeremiah had found *you* in Jerusalem, would God have spared the city? _____

Why? _____

_____

What are the three most important changes you need to make in the context of today's devotional?

1. _____

2. _____

3. _____

Day 3

Penalty Box

So Miriam was confined outside the
camp for seven days, and the people did not
move on till she was brought back.
Numbers 12:15 (NIV)

Observation: Miriam had exposed a petulant jealous streak by speaking against Moses, saying, "Has the Lord spoken only through Moses? Hasn't He also spoken through us?" (Num. 12:2). Angered, God struck Miriam with leprosy. Moses immediately interceded for her, but God required that she bear her uncleanness by being put outside the camp for seven days, a very public rebuke.

Application: The Lord has a deft touch indeed as he reveals our heart condition through a simple story several thousand years old. Miriam was beloved of God; she also led the nation in exuberant celebration after their Red Sea deliverance from Pharaoh's army (see Ex. 15:20–21). The prophet Micah would later remind of God's having "sent Moses to lead [the nation], also Aaron and Miriam" (Micah 6:4, NIV). She was honored, famous, and secure in God's love.

Yet Miriam, like me, was apparently still capable of blurting things she would regret, words that revealed an area of her heart not yet fully yielded to God. The resulting discipline, while due to her sin, was nonetheless motivated by God's love for her and for those around her. As long as she was in the penalty box, forward progress waited. It is in the goodness of God, not meanness, that the time finally comes for Him to address heart issues I would prefer to leave buried. In my headlong rush to achieve something, to become something, my loving Abba will design a penalty box just my size: a major illness, a business reversal, a relational train wreck, or some other creative invention.

There comes a time when God determines that this thing is to be addressed now, no longer to be hidden from view, covered by pretense. He calls "time out," and like Miriam, I find that forward progress stops while He works on my heart. I must see this not as the harsh punishment of an angry God, but as a necessary course correction by the lover of my soul. He is much more committed to my intimacy with Him than He is to the outer accoutrements I have given my life to pursue. After all, He Himself volunteered for the shame of the Cross; He would appear to have been a failure in his earthly ministry. Should I think myself above the suffering to which He submitted? Love put Miriam outside the camp. And it is His passionate love for me that has caused me to join her there.

Prayer: O Lord, when I see You through the paradigm of a lovesick bridegroom rather than as a cranky, harsh, disapproving authority, the hard things in life take on new meaning. Thank You for loving me enough to crush me when it is needed. I gladly submit to Your work in my heart.

Consider:

What words have you spoken in the distant past that may still have you in a penalty box? _____

_____

_____

What about the last two weeks? _____

_____

_____

What steps do you plan to take today to regain your freedom?
1. _____
2. _____
3. _____

Day 4

PLUNDERING THE ENEMY

And he carried out from there all the treasures of
the house of the LORD, and the treasures of the
kings house, and
cut in pieces all the vessels of gold which Solomon
king of Israel had made
in the temple of the LORD.
2 KINGS 24:13

Observation: The king of Babylon had just taken captive the king of Judah and all the royal family. Naturally, all the treasures of the temple were also taken, including the vessels of gold made by Solomon for temple worship. See how temporary and easily undone are even the best works of man? The people of Solomon's day had rallied with supernatural fervor to give generously to the construction of the temple, and for its vessels. Yet now, many kings later, all that had been built by godly leaders and obedient people was sitting in the treasury of the enemy.

By contrast, consider Psalm 112, which speaks of the permanence of God's blessings for those who fear Him. Their righteousness will be established and will endure forever. No amount of evil tidings will bring fear to their hearts; rather, their hearts will remain steadfast.

Application: What is the difference between these two passages? David's psalm about everlasting fruit flowing from the life of a righteous man must be squared against the reality that the fruit of his son Solomon's reign would one day enrich the treasury of the enemy. How can I be confident that the treasure of my life will have eternally meaningful impact?

An important part of the answer is to simply deny responsibility for how those in the future steward their own lives. There is undeniable truth here; I cannot force my physical or spiritual progeny to come to Christ and be filled with His Spirit, let alone govern the righteousness of their daily walk. But it is also true that the firmer the foundation of my own life, the greater the likelihood that the enemy's treasuries may never be filled with booty from the lives of my loved ones.

Prayer: Holy Spirit, I ask You for a fresh infilling this morning. Refresh my supply of oil, Lord, that I might be well equipped to not only be a useful tool in Your hands for today, but also that I might leave a lasting legacy upon which others can build. Fill my children with Your Spirit, Lord. Cause my physical and my spiritual family to today put down roots deep into You.

Consider:

Which of your treasures have been put at risk recently? _____
_____
_____

What has this loss revealed about the foundation of your faith?
_____
_____
_____

How might your response be adjusted to help protect future generations from the enemy's plundering? _____
_____
_____
_____

Day 5

A Useful Test

Your threshing will continue until grape harvest
and the grape harvest will continue until planting,
and you will be eating
all the food you want. . . . You will still be eating
last year's harvest when you have
to move it out to make room for the new.
Leviticus 26:5, 10 (NIV)

Observation: Leviticus 26 is the first place to extensively describe contrasts between those who walk in obedience and those who do not. It begins with God saying that if his people would follow His decrees, He would send rain in its season causing the ground to yield its crops and the trees to produce fruit. As if to drive home the idea of a never-ending provision, He said the harvests would be so plentiful that they'd have to move out the old to make room for the new; one harvest would extend to the next, and they would never know hunger.

Application: Think of it: a supply so abundant I would never go hungry! A God-given buffet stretching as far as the eye can see, through every season of need. In this passage, the idea of His provision is that I will find myself living under His constant, generous outpouring, like being surrounded by snowflakes in an unending blizzard.

Do I really believe that? Was it good for the Hebrews but holds no application to my life today? If I say I believe His promise, does my lifestyle put the lie to my words? It is one thing for the poor of the earth to trust in such promises. They have no opportunity to step into my shoes, accumulating for themselves great stores of capital from which to live. The poor have little choice but to rely on a daily provision—manna falling from heaven or an agency handout.

But I who am rich ought to consider if, by laying up more wealth than needed for my daily supply, I have begun inching toward a role of self-provision that God intended for Himself. Have I crossed a line from being God-dependent, to the cultish view that I will become a god myself?

Here is a useful little test. Settle into a quiet place and imagine that all your capital assets have suddenly been taken away: 401(k), life insurance, nice home, well-paying job. Understand that you are now utterly dependent upon God for all daily provision. What passes through mind and heart in that moment? Is it terror and fear, or is there a deep assurance that He will keep all His promises? Does the mind begin to nervously consider whether I have kept my end of the bargain, keeping the first commandment first in all things? Am I glad to throw myself upon Him for every need?

Prayer: Father, this useful test has helped to reveal the focus of my own confidence. Forgive me, Lord, for saying I trust You, yet living another way. Make me into a delighted dependent of Your outpouring.

Consider:

Who have you credited for any financial success you have had? Your own hard work, or God's grace? _____

If God is credited, does He have the right to take away what He provided? _____

_____

Why? _____

_____

_____

Day 6

AMBLE PAST THE CEMETERY

Have You come here to torment us before the time?
MATTHEW 8:29

Observation: As Jesus passed a cemetery, two demon-possessed men confronted him. They were so crazed that locals avoided that section of road. The demons within these men instantly recognized the Savior; they knew His authority, and they knew their own destiny as demonstrated by their loud cry, "Have You come here to torment us before the time?" Before what time? Those demons knew their place, and they thought they could occupy it for a little longer, but they also knew a time was coming when all would change. In an age to come there would be a season of judgment, when the fruit of our lives will be ripe, and we will have our rewards based upon what we have done with the claims of Christ.

Application: No conceivable thought is more terrifying than to look into the future and know we are doomed to hear, "Depart from Me!" (Matt. 7:23). This is what the demons dreaded, for they knew full well it was deserved. Their objection was not over their destination, but over His timing; their end seemed to come sooner than they had assumed. They had been confident that the Son of God would delay a bit longer.

What goes through my mind as I think about these two sorry demons? "You'll get yours! You deserve whatever God has in store for you! How can you be so blind, so stupid?" But somewhere between "blind" and "stupid," the tumble of thoughts slows a bit as the idea intrudes that I, too, have been as they were. I know my destiny; it is a wedding banquet.

But as good as all that is, I sometimes struggle over the timing of destiny's fulfillment. That struggle is rooted in only one thing:

reluctance to fully abandon pursuits other than Him. I want to teeter on the edge of sin, seeing how many ways my heart can be divided while casting one eye nervously toward the eastern sky, planning against all odds to instantly abandon worldly pursuits when I see Him beginning to split the heavens. But here's the problem: when He comes, He'll probably be really quick about it. First Corinthians 15:52 says in a moment, in an eye's twinkling, everything will be changed. He won't be on a slow amble past the cemetery next time; rather, He will come for His bride quicker than a blink. Will my response be any different from the demons', "Lord, have You come here . . . before the time?"

Prayer: Lord Jesus, Your timing is perfect, and it is unknowable. I repent, Lord, of every scrap of unfinished heart business, every tendency to linger over habits and patterns of life that keep me from wholehearted pursuit of You. Stir zeal for You, O Lord, for You alone.

Consider:

When loss comes, do you complain about its timing or welcome it as a helpful chance for course correction from God? _____

_____

Why? _____

_____

_____

_____

_____

_____

_____

Day 7

COMPLETE WETNESS

For the earth will be filled with the knowledge
of the glory of the LORD, as the waters cover
the sea. . . . Though the fig tree should not blossom and
there be no fruit on the vines,
though the yield of the olive should fail and the fields
produce no food, though the flocks should
be cut off from the fold and there be
no cattle in the stalls, yet I will exult in the LORD;
I will rejoice in the God of my salvation.

HABAKKUK 2:14; 3:17-18

Observation: It is clear that Habakkuk passionately loved God. He prophesied judgment on sinful Judah, yet he also broke out in praise the likes of which is hardly found in the Old Testament outside the psalms. His simile in 2:14 stretches language as though seeking to convey never-before-imagined meaning: that the knowledge of the glory of the Lord would so fill the earth that it would be like water covering the sea.

Application: Is there anywhere on the sea that is not water? Can there be found any nook or cranny of the sea without the wetness of water covering it? Of course not! And just as this perfect physical example of complete coverage soaks my mind and heart, so am I to understand that nowhere on earth will be found even the tiniest hiding place unsaturated with the knowledge of the glory of the Lord. Habakkuk uses other similes to declare his heart commitment to praise and trust God. Imagine no fruit from fig or olive trees. Picture no flocks or herds anywhere in the world. Yet even in the direst circumstances, Habakkuk will exult in God.

Talk about challenging me to rise above my circumstances! These verses are a wonderful reminder to re-examine all that I hope in, all that I put my trust in. What a sweet, awful responsibility.

Prayer: I pray, Father, that You would deliver me from any focus on outward circumstances as the basis for evaluating my life and the times in which I live. I have had trials, yet You have met every need. There have been reasons to be fainthearted, yet You have delivered me in the midst of every trial. The times are evil, yet Your goodness fills my heart to overflowing, and I rejoice in Your salvation. Cause great rejoicing to burst forth in my heart as Your spirit fills me with the knowledge of the glory of the Holy One! Bless the name of Jesus!

Consider:

Do you still exult in God in the midst of financial challenges?

_____

_____

Do you find it easier or more difficult to praise Him in tough circumstances? _____

_____

Why? _____

_____

_____

_____

_____

_____

Day 8

CONFUSING ROLES

When the LORD your God cuts off the nations,
whose land the LORD your God gives you and
. . . if the LORD your God enlarges your
territory, . . . and gives you all the land which
He promised . . .if you carefully observe all this
commandment . . . to love the LORD your God and
to walk in His ways always . . .

DEUTERONOMY 19:1, 8–9

Observation: The Lord was describing His plan to give the Israelites all the land promised them, and even more, so there would be plenty of cities of refuge. The magnificent sweep of His promises was that if obeyed, He would be surpassingly generous in response.

Application: In the course of relating His promises to the people, God makes clear that there is a division of labor in His economy. God has a role, and I have a role. His part is to do the warring to cut off His enemies, to defeat every foe so my territory can be enlarged. My part is to possess what He has made available, and to love Him and to walk in His ways.

How often I confuse my role with God's. Is it the responsibility of an employee to see that the rent is paid, equipment purchased, supplies laid in for the day's work? Of course not. That is the responsibility of the owner, properly delegated. Still, when I survey what seems to have been laid before me, it seems I must be quarterback, receiver, and blocker as I rush the goal. But that is never God's intent. He is the owner; it is His job to plan, His job to run interference so each play will delight with its apparent ease.

My problem is that I grow impatient or conclude that I know better than He what needs to happen. So I try to assume His responsibility, warring in the flesh, mistaking presumption for great faith. Whenever I do that, I am actually operating in a lack of faith, because I do not trust Him to do what He has said He would do.

Prayer: Father, teach me to wait upon You, to be content in Your timing. Your resources are more than sufficient to win every battle, so when it seems that I am losing, when I see myself sinking like Peter did as he walked on the water, remind me, Lord, that the battle is Yours, and cause me to learn what You want me to learn while going through Your process. I choose to sit at Your feet, focusing on Your beauty, waiting on You, yearning to become one with You in every way. I love You, Lord.

Consider:

How have you confused your role with God's in thinking about your financial security? _____

_____

_____

_____

_____

What steps can you take to bring needed course correction?
1. _____
2. _____
3. _____

Who will you ask to hold you accountable? _____

_____

Day 9

FLESHLY NAVIGATION

When a moderate south wind came up, supposing
that they had attained their purpose, they
weighed anchor and began sailing.
ACTS 27:13

Observation: Paul was prisoner on a ship sailing for Rome under difficult circumstances. Never one to ignore an audience, Paul, though in chains, gave warning to the experienced seamen that great danger lay ahead if they pressed on. Naturally, the men chose to ignore Paul's advice and to trust instead in their years of sailing acumen. Within ten verses, they had encountered such dire circumstances that all hope of surviving was abandoned, all because they chose to follow a moderate south wind rather than the warning from God.

Application: The crew supposed they had gained their purpose. Such a small phrase, yet one laden with truth as a commentary on how I all too often govern my life. The ship was at risk because they chose to trust their accumulated years of experience to get them to safe harbor. They acted in presumption.

Isn't this a perfect picture of men exalting themselves above God? They had clear warning against proceeding, but they trusted in their own prowess for deliverance, and it ended in near catastrophe. Perhaps they arrogantly considered the source of the warnings—a man in chains heading for trial in Rome—and decided he could not possibly have important information to share. In any event, a modest south wind came up, so off they went.

How foolish, yet how like me. I ignore clear but inconvenient warnings, thinking my abilities will carry me safely through. As a consequence, I look for a moderate south wind and leap to catch its advantage. But I proceed at my own peril. I feverishly crunch the numbers to set the course of business, asking God to bless my efforts. I rely upon generational experience to raise children, ignoring hard teachings of Scripture. In deciding that I know better than God what is best, I learn gradually to ignore and ultimately to extinguish the quietly pleading voice of God that would lead into all wisdom. But God doesn't abandon me; He merely requires a course correction. He says, as Paul would tell the people, not to be afraid. Yes, the ship is going to founder, but God will preserve you. He will rescue you if you will obey His voice and turn from the course chosen by fleshly navigation (see Acts 27:22–25).

Prayer: Father God, there is nothing within me that merits Your favor, yet You have granted it nonetheless. You stand at the ready, eager for me finally to follow You rather than my own inclinations. Thank You, Lord, that You are wringing earthly desires out of me and gradually teaching me to hear and obey Your voice.

Consider:

How have you acted in financial presumption? _____
_____
_____

What has been its effect on you and/or your family? _____
_____
_____

What are the three most important lessons learned from this experience?
1. _____
2. _____
3. _____

Day 10

KNOWING HIS TIMING

This is the day the LORD spoke of when He said to
you, "I will give your enemy into
your hands to deal with as you wish."
1 SAMUEL 24:4 (NIV)

Observation: Saul has gone into a cave, apparently to rest from midday heat, unaware that David and some of his men were themselves hidden within. Seeing Saul at rest and realizing this was a unique opportunity for David to kill Saul, David's men urged him to take action, justifying it by claiming it's what God intended by orchestrating these remarkable circumstances.

Application: Perhaps the first thing we ought to note about verse 4 is that David's men were flat wrong; God had never said He would give Saul into David's hands for David to do with as he wished. God had indeed on several occasions given David a promise to one day lead the nation; He had also assured David that the kingdom would one day be taken from Saul. While these promises had surely expanded David's heart with vision, his men were seriously overreaching in their misrepresentation of what God had actually said.

The second and perhaps more important thing to understand about the story is that even knowing God's general plan for David's life still left him in the dark as to its timing. Had David acted to take Saul's life he would have been fulfilling God's promise in the flesh. Rather than waiting for God's perfect timing, David's acceleration of the implementation of God's plan would surely have turned intended blessing into an agonizing source of regret for the rest of David's days.

How easy it is to project myself into this story. Sadly, though, I would often best fit the role of David's men, rather than that of

David. In innumerable ways, God has been gracious to reveal wonderful promises to my heart. Just to know that the God who created the vastness of the heavens deigns even to consider me is a daily astonishment; to know He actually intends good for me rather than evil is beyond comprehension.

My shortcoming is this: having some sense of His promises for my life, I assume He must intend them for now. Today. "Seize the moment," my heart cries! Make it happen. In such presumption I am almost always wrong. David was wise enough to understand that God's timing is not always revealed as clearly as is God's plan. He had spent enough time contemplating the beauty and majesty of God to know that if God had ordained some good thing for his life, He was perfectly capable of bringing it about in His perfect timing.

Prayer: Father, I shudder in self-disappointment when I think of my presumption in believing that I knew Your timing as well as Your promise. Forgive me for moving ahead of what You have clearly revealed. Cause me to wait in contentment upon You.

Consider:

Name an instance in which you were confident of God's plan for you, yet you sought its fulfillment in your own timing. _____

_____

_____

What were the consequences? _____

_____

_____

How did you/will you correct the situation? _____

_____

_____

Day 11

PERFECT TRUST

For You, O LORD of Hosts, the God of Israel,
have made a revelation to Your servant, saying
'I will build you a house'; therefore Your servant
has found courage to pray this prayer to You. And
now O Lord GOD, You are God and Your words
are truth, and You have promised this good thing
to Your servant. Now therefore may it please You
to bless the house of Your servant, that it may
continue forever before You. For You, O Lord
GOD, have spoken; and with Your blessing may the
house of Your servant be blessed forever.

2 SAMUEL 7:27–29

Observation: Chapter 7 of 2 Samuel depicts David's unquestioning trust in the Lord. It begins with his well-intentioned and generous impulse to build a permanent house of God, and initially the prophet Nathan affirms David's desire. Then God speaks something radically different. God says that instead of David's building a house for Him, He will instead build a house for David, referring to the dynasty of kings flowing from David that would ultimately produce King Jesus.

Application: David so trusted what he heard from God that he was settled, content in it. God's promise was "to" David and "about" David and his lineage, but it was a promise that David knew he would not live to see fulfilled. Yet David's trust was so complete that he could treat it as something already accomplished. He was so settled in trusting God's promise as to lay down completely his heart's dream of being the one to build a physical house for God.

This speaks in a profound way of the need to lay down my own vision for my life, regardless of how much I may feel my path is

God-breathed. I will never forget a time, many years ago now, when my wife Cindy and I were dealing with the reality of a major flare-up of her MS. Several men in Austin, Texas, prayed over me regarding "unfulfilled expectations." As they spoke, it was as though floodgates of my soul opened, and all those dreams and expectations I held seemed to be washed away in an on-rushing flood of God's love.

His provision for me is more than enough. His purposes for my life are exactly right. He is teaching me to be content in Him, and to go to sleep each night, like David, knowing that God will absolutely accomplish what He has promised, whether I live to see it or not.

Prayer: Lord Jesus, thank You for planting new expectations in my heart—expectations of You and what You will accomplish in me and in the lives of those I love. Have Your way with me, Lord.

Consider:

What is the biggest unfulfilled financial expectation of your life?

_____

_____

_____

How have you dealt with it? _____

_____

_____

_____

What steps still need to be taken? _____

_____

_____

_____

Day 12

SHORTCOMINGS OF LOINCLOTHS

Then the eyes of both of them were opened,
and they knew that they were naked;
and they sewed fig leaves together and made
themselves loin coverings.
Genesis 3:7

Observation: Sin had been firmly established through the disobedience of Adam and Eve. Having eaten from the tree of the knowledge of good and evil, they gained knowledge as their understanding was opened to their nakedness. Since they lived with both the immediate and the long-term consequences of sin, they viewed their nakedness with shame rather than delight, and took steps to cover themselves from one another.

Application: Sin is an awful bedfellow, but in our natural condition it is inescapable. Its consequences are often immediate, always long-term, and unfailingly horrific. The Word says that as Adam and Eve understood their nakedness, they sewed fig leaves together to make themselves loin coverings. In this we must see that they traded God's covering for a covering they made themselves.

Every aspect of the story is tragic, but none more than this. God's covering had brought peace and fellowship with Him and delight in one another and in their surroundings. They were soon to be expelled from Eden, sentenced to earn their living by sweat, to bear children in pain, and to live with the loss of intimacy with God. Their own covering was a poor substitute indeed, a false covering which necessarily led to a false identity.

"I can do it myself! I must try harder or work smarter. I'll have to get up earlier to get a jump on our competitors. I'll be watching next time, ready for any funny business they might try." The man or woman who has for a covering their own ingenuity, their own capabilities, is in deep trouble. We get our identity from our covering, and there are only two possible sources: from God or from the place where Adam shopped. Take this challenge: go to the loincloth department of the finest clothing store in town. The best they have will still permit the cold, chilling updraft of reality to blow in. And beloved, even the freshest of fig leaves will soon dry and crumble.

Terror of exposure will dog me all my days until I at last confess that I must come under a more substantial covering. I need a cleft in an immovable Rock in which to hide, not the vagaries of a loin covering of my own making. Christ gave His life to purchase me for His kingdom, whom He found pitiably cowering behind fig leaves of my own design. He again offers the open doors of Eden. Will I be wise enough to enter into Him?

Prayer: Lord Jesus, all the striving in the world leaves me exhausted and failed. Thank You for reestablishing Your covering over me, and for the peace and rest I find there.

Consider:

With regard to finances, what fake coverings have you bought into?

_____

_____

How have they impacted you and those you love? _____

_____

_____

How should you now respond? _____

_____

_____

Day 13

STAR PEGS AND ROUND HOLES

Blessed is he who does not take offense at Me.
MATTHEW 11:6

Observation: The evil king Herod, who was in an illegitimate relationship with his wife, Herodias, had imprisoned John the Baptist. John had called them on it. Even though Herod was intrigued by John and enjoyed his preaching, Herodias hated John and demanded his beheading. Just before his execution, John sent followers to ask Jesus if He was the Messiah they had been waiting for. John already knew the answer; his faith was unshakable. He had baptized Jesus in the desert and saw God's spirit descending from heaven. He was the forerunner, the one Scripture called a burning lamp (see John 5:35). But some of his followers had not yet fully embraced Jesus; they were too attached to John, so John sent them to get a personal word from Jesus. What Jesus said struck to the innermost places of intimacy in their hearts. After reminding them of the astonishing array of miracles He had performed, He said, "Blessed is he who does not take offense at Me."

Application: Jesus was saying in effect: Guys, I know why you have come. You want Me to set John free from prison; you want Me to prevent his beheading. I love John, but it is his time to decrease, and My time to increase. Though I have the power to free him, I'm not going to do it. This will be a profound test of your hearts as to whether you stumble over Me. Every offendable heart will be offended.

Who among us has not watched with bemusement as a small boy works intently to press a star-shaped peg into a round hole? Pushing, concentrating mightily, every thwarted attempt produces greater frustration, greater determination to create an impossible result. Such toddler ways are alive within me, as within John's disciples. Determined to have my way, I keep on pushing, trying to manipulate things to produce an outcome that is not to be. I may grow frustrated to the point of petulance, even anger; I may throw the hammer in frustration or even kick the toy, but at the end of the day I will still not have my way; stars do not fit into circles.

Jesus urges me instead to be at peace, to rest in Him. The door to peace and contentment in Him will never come through successful manipulation. In Him alone there is rest and fullness of joy. I am called to lay down my poor toys—hopes, dreams, and expectations apart from Him. "Blessed is he who does not take offense at Me."

Prayer: Lord Jesus, You wait patiently for me to stop striving, to be at peace in You and You alone. Forgive me for thinking I must have something more than You to be content. Forgive me all those times I have tried to determine the outcome of a thing, to manipulate You to my supposed advantage. You are enough, Lord, more than enough.

Consider:

In light of your financial circumstances, how have you stumbled in offense against God?

What do you need to do differently now?

Day 14

STEEPED IN FAITH'S TRADITIONS

But they laughed at Him.
MARK 5:40 (NIV)

Observation: Jairus, an administrator of the local synagogue, had asked Jesus to lay hands on his dying twelve-year-old daughter. Meanwhile, at the house, mournful wails accompanying death had already begun. Jesus and Jairus were too late, so messengers came from the house to find Jairus on the way. Since his daughter had already died, there was no need to further trouble the Master. Jesus, though, overrode their message by simply saying, "Don't be afraid; just believe" (Mark 5:36), as they continued toward the house. Then, upon arriving and hearing the shrill mourners, He asked, "Why all this commotion and wailing? The child is not dead, but asleep" (v. 39), to which they responded by laughing at Him.

Application: The crowd's reaction to Jesus was in marked contrast to that of some demons earlier in the chapter. A demoniac living among tombs outside the town had run toward Jesus. As he ran, the primary demon possessing the man began a deadly earnest dialogue with Jesus. The demons recognized Jesus's authority, and His presence was no laughing matter to them! The demons begged Jesus "again and again" not to send them away (v. 10).

By contrast, the good believers at Jairus's house dared to laugh at the Son of God. They thought they knew death when they saw it, and Jairus's daughter had been dead long enough for a crowd of mourners to assemble. What's going on here? Jairus's crowd had plenty of information about Jesus. They understood He could do anything. As synagogue administrator, Jairus surely would have been steeped in faith's traditions, and he apparently had enough knowledge of Jesus's reputation to have been willing to ask Him to lay hands on his daughter in the first place. Yet it was his family and friends who laughed at Jesus, while the demons had trembled in fear before Him.

Is my faith only good on sunny summer afternoons with soft breezes blowing? What of those darker days when gale-force winds bring awful news crashing in? She's dead. You're fired. He has left you for another woman. She's pregnant. He was so full of cancer they just sewed him back up. We're out of money. You flunked the test. The list of possible bad news is unimaginably long, and there are days, even years, when it seems to come in double or triple doses. What is my response on such a day? Dare I join in the jeering crowd at Jairus's house, or might I have at least the wisdom of a minor demon?

Prayer: Lord Jesus, forgive me for the times I have responded as Jairus's friends. When all the niceties are stripped away, when life is reduced to my heart response to Your presence in the midst of a storm, I pray You would find me trusting only in You, believing You, satisfied fully by You.

Consider:

What bad news do you most fear? _____

_____

What has been the worst bad news actually fulfilled in your life?

_____

How did you respond? _____

_____

In light of this devotional, how might you adjust your response going forward? _____

_____

Day 15

Timing Is the Hard Part

Am I in the place of God, who has kept you
from having children?
Genesis 30:2 (NIV)

Observation: Jacob had set off on the task of siring twelve sons, each of whom would become head of one of the tribes of Israel. Although Rachel was the favored wife, it was through her sister, Leah, that the first four were born as Rachel fumed through her barrenness. In desperate jealousy, Rachel cried to Jacob, "Give me children, or I'll die," (Gen. 30:1, NIV) which elicited Jacob's angry response: "Am I in the place of God?"

Application: When this question appears in the midst of the story of God's founding of the nation of Israel, it is hard to imagine the words coming from Jacob's lips. Perhaps at long last he has learned to ask the right question.

As a young man Jacob had extorted the birthright of his older brother Esau through the price of one savory meal. Later, Jacob and his mother had connived to trick the dying Isaac into granting Jacob the generational blessing that should have been Esau's. There is apparently nothing in Jacob to suggest he would later know how to hear God's voice or harbor the inclination to wait on His timing. Nevertheless, Jacob had landed where God intended. After all, before the birth of twins Esau and Jacob, the Lord had said to Rebekah, "Two nations are in your womb; . . . one people will be stronger than the other; and the older will serve the younger" (Gen. 25:23, NIV).

God cares not only that I get the thing right, but that I get the timing and method right as well. It is sin to determine my destiny apart from God, but it is equally wrong when, having heard from Him as to my future, I then seize its fulfillment in my own timing, my own way, my own strength. Timing can be tricky. The man who, for example, says he wants to spend his retirement fund down to zero the day he dies illustrates the problem. He understands the purpose of the money, but knowing the day to calendar its depletion reminds of the Grey Lines guide showing his patrons the Chicago alley where a murdered mobster was found with 27 cents in his pocket, whereupon one of the patrons remarked, "What great timing!" When God has spoken to me about a thing, does it remain His if its fulfillment comes in my timing, by my schemes? He has authored a good and perfect plan for each of us. How great will be my joy when the fruit of my life is His in every way. I must press in, wait on Him, then press in some more.

Prayer: Lord Jesus, thank You that the plans You have for me are to prosper me, and not to harm me, plans to give me hope, and a future. Cause me to seek You with all my heart, Lord, that the fruit of my life will be pleasing to You in every way.

Consider:

Think of an instance where you were certain of God's intention to bless you and you rushed ahead to implement it in your own strength. What were the results? _____

_____

_____

_____

_____

_____

_____

Day 16

Which Burden Shall It Be?

The things that you carry are burdensome, a load for
the weary beast. They stooped over, they
have bowed down together, and they could not rescue
the burden but have gone into captivity
together. . . . Listen to Me, . . . you who have been borne
by Me from birth and have been
carried from the womb. Even to your old age I will be the
same, and even to your graying years
I will bear you. I have done it, and I will carry you; and I
will bear you and I will deliver you.

Isaiah 46:1–4

Observation: God here contrasted Himself with those who carry around their own burdens. Without Him, men make their own images of wood and stone to worship, creating lifestyles that are burdensome indeed. In such circumstances we are weighted down by having to carry all this "stuff" ourselves. We become exhausted trying to maintain the big house and expensive toys, burdens which God never intended us to carry. In Isaiah 46:3–4, the contrast could not be more profound: God said that He carries the burden of His beloved people, that He is faithful and able to carry the load.

Application: This is such a hopeful passage! Oh to have a clear understanding of the contrast God presents here. I put myself under an impossibly heavy load when I try to go my own way in life, yet it seems so easy at the beginning of the journey. What could be simpler than to set my own standards for living, apart from the supposedly "heavy" demands of God?

Yet the opposite is true. God is here saying that He has been carrying me since I was in my mother's womb, and that He will remain faithful to carry me even to old age. My part in this is to simply lay my burden down and to enter into His life, His plan for me. He is both committed and able to carry me through every circumstance of life. His supernatural hand of protection has indeed been over me; His deliverance is sure. All I need do is to finally, at long last, surrender. I bring nothing of value to the table; my life is His, and I am content to be carried by Him.

Prayer: Lord Jesus, the yoke You put on me is so easy to bear compared to the heavy burdens of life I fashion for myself to carry. Forgive me for those times when I have stooped low to pick up heavy loads that You have not required of me. I choose today to rest in You. I choose to simplify my life and to experience the joy of being carried along by You to that awesome wedding feast that awaits.

Consider:

How has your life become weighted down by carrying too much "stuff" around? _____

_____

_____

_____

What steps is God requiring of you now? _____

_____

_____

_____

How do you feel about that? _____

_____

_____

_____

Day 17

EARLY HIRES

But he answered one of them, "Friend, I am not
being unfair to you. Didn't you
agree to work for a denarius?"
Matthew 20:13 (NIV)

Observation: This verse is found within the familiar story of workers hired to labor in a vineyard. Some had been hired early in the morning to work all day for a denarius. Several more times as the day advanced, the owner hired additional men; at day's end, the foremen distributed wages of one denarius to each man regardless of the length of his workday. The early hires objected to their one-denarius paycheck, claiming it was unfair that others who worked less should be paid the same. But the owner reminded them that there was no unfairness in what they were paid; their wage was exactly as promised at the beginning of their engagement.

Application: Whose side seems right in this exchange? Upon careful reflection, we must confess that the owner is exactly right in what he says to the early hires. Doesn't he indeed have the right to pay each laborer whatever he wishes for their work?

While it may be easy to concede the owner's correct response, doesn't the heart tend toward sympathy with the complaint of the early hires? Despite their agreement to work all day for a denarius, doesn't something within us empathize with their emotions? Perhaps that is because we too readily think as they think.

When I came to Christ as a single man, there was a time when I declared to God that He alone was more than enough. Each of us, if we have experienced genuine conversion, must have said something akin to that.

Why then, when I see an elderly couple holding hands do I feel pangs of envy as I recall my too-young wife now dead? I must ask myself: Did I mean it when I told the Lord that He is more than enough? For the childless couple struggling with empty playgrounds in their mind, or the family that has lost son or daughter prematurely, thinking of birthdays uncelebrated and grandchildren unborn, the question must be answered afresh. Did I mean it when I said Christ is sufficient? It is in life's empty moments that I must remember my hiring wage—one denarius for a day's work, regardless of what others receive. In that breathtaking moment hangs my destiny, to linger in loss and disappointment or to confess again that He is more than enough.

Prayer: Lord Jesus, You know each time I have responded like a worker claiming mistreatment. Forgive me, Lord. You are eternally just and righteous in Your provision for my life.

Consider:

Is God indeed enough? _____

_____

In what areas of your life do you struggle most in answering this question? _____

_____

_____

_____

Why? _____

_____

_____

_____

Day 18

ELEVATOR MANNERS

When you take a census of the sons of Israel to
number them, then each one of them
shall give a ransom for himself to the LORD,
when you number them, so that there
will be no plague among them. . . . Everyone
who is numbered, from twenty years old
and over, shall give the contribution
to the LORD. The rich shall not pay more and the
poor shall not pay less than the half shekel,
when you give the contribution to the LORD to
make atonement for yourselves.
EXODUS 30:12, 14–15

Observation: This passage is about money given for atonement for sin. It is part of a much larger passage of instructions on how to build the altar and how Aaron is to use it to make atonement for sin using the blood of the sin offering.

Application: Isn't it interesting that the price for atonement was identical for everybody? Rich and poor alike had to pay the same price, demonstrating again that His sacrifice, not ours, provided the redemption for all of us, equally (see 1 Pet. 3:18).

How often do I allow myself to begin thinking how great a prize I am in God's kingdom? How pleased He must be with my performance here or my effectiveness there! I'm sure He noticed the significant check I recently gave; perhaps He will have someone erect a sort of memorial in my honor. And I hope He noticed the time last week when I so graciously yielded to that person frantic to board the elevator.

I can begin to think that God must place a higher value on me than He does on, say, an Asian tsunami victim. I think that because I am clean, because I dress well, or because of where I live, God must surely have been "extra glad" to have redeemed me. Nothing could be farther from the truth.

Prayer: Lord, You are the great equalizer. In Your presence, no one can stand. My best righteousness is like dirty rags compared to Your glory and majesty. Father, there is nothing I can bring to You by which I can be made worthy. I am like every other man or woman in Your sight, fallen and sinful and desperately in need of the redemption that can only come through the sacrifice of Your dear Son.

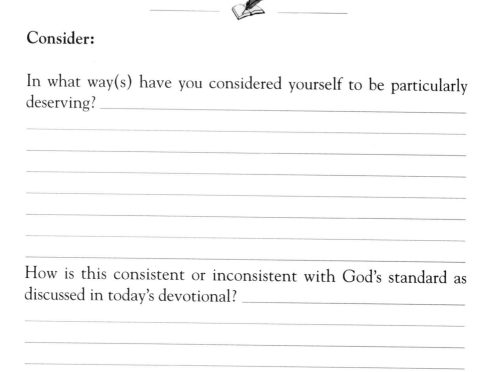

Consider:

In what way(s) have you considered yourself to be particularly deserving? _____

_____

_____

_____

_____

_____

_____

How is this consistent or inconsistent with God's standard as discussed in today's devotional? _____

_____

_____

_____

_____

Day 19

AFRICAN FIELD HAND

The more the priests increased, the more they
sinned against me; they exchanged their
Glory for something disgraceful.
HOSEA 4:7 (NIV)

Observation: Through the prophet Hosea, God condemned both the nation of Israel and their priests. They had rejected knowledge, so God had rejected them (Hosea 4:6) The priests, Hosea said, have fed "on the sins of my people and relish their wickedness" (v.8) In their unfaithfulness to God, they have been led astray by a spirit of prostitution (v.12). Then comes the summary indictment: "They exchanged their Glory for something disgraceful."

Application: Israel and her priests had a small beginning; they started out modest in size and wealth, but had grown tremendously over the generations. God's love and blessing had brought them great wealth and power, but with increased blessing had come increased sin. As affluence and power increased, they had fallen away from God. With national prominence, military victory, and increasing creature comforts had come self-reliance and disgusting indulgences.

Their glory flowed directly from God's blessing. It was by His grace that they had grown in number, wealth, and power. These were her glory, yet see how far Israel was about to fall.

We are never more vulnerable than in a season of great accomplishment. That financial pinnacle we've worked hard to gain, the important military accomplishment, the winning season after a long dry spell—these successes bring glory, yet the danger is this: it is from such heights that the severest fall is possible.

Danger lies in my tendency to revel in such glories, forgetting that they are simply the fruit of God's sovereign grace in my life. I may have worked hard in pursuit of some important goal, but it is arrogance to presume success is my right; might not a poor laborer with a hoe in the African sun have labored far more? That African field hand may well find himself in a more right relationship with God than the wealthiest corporate titan. Then who is the impoverished one? Whose future should I prefer?

Ultimately, I run the risk of being counted among the priests addressed by Hosea, for if I dishonor God in the midst of His abundant blessing, then that very blessing becomes my shame. The writer of 1 Samuel 2:30 (NIV) got it just right when he said, "Those who honor me I will honor, but those who despise me will be disdained."

Prayer: Lord, You keep drawing me back to dependence upon You, where You challenge me to be content. Your grace has produced much undeserved glory in my life. Keep me ever mindful of glory's Source.

Consider:

Give an example of a financial pinnacle from which you have fallen. _____

_____

_____

_____

How has it changed your view of financial security? _____

_____

_____

_____

Day 20

CHASING HER TAIL

Therefore I will block her path with
thornbushes; I will wall her in so that she
cannot find her way. She will chase after her
lovers but not catch them; she will look
for them but not find them.

HOSEA 2:6–7 (NIV)

Observation: Israel is portrayed as an unfaithful wife bearing illegitimate children (v. 5) in alliances that can never satisfy. She is shown crediting her success to false lovers rather than acknowledging that it was her husband (God) who had miraculously and faithfully provided her every need. In response, God declares that He will wall her in, making it impossible for her to dally with the lovers she so avidly pursues.

Application: Think for a moment about the profound protection God offers to His beloved. She will not be permitted to find satisfaction in other than Him. Her repeated trysts with substitute lovers will be thwarted. No matter how frantic her efforts to pursue self-debasing relationships, God's sovereign love will captivate her for her own good.

The Word says, "She will chase after her lovers but not catch them," conjuring an image of a dog fruitlessly pursuing its tail. Perpetually unsuccessful, she seems nevertheless not to tire of the effort.

What is it about the human heart that causes it to seek satisfaction other than in God? Why, against all evidence to the contrary, do we live as though this is our home, and that our chief end is to achieve success as the world measures such things?

It is embarrassing to admit to all the tails I have chased over the years, growling and barking as I circled in unrequited pursuit of "treasures on earth where moth and rust destroy" (Matthew 6:19). But more embarrassing still, even shameful, is the honest confession that the tendency toward such pursuits has not yet been fully wrung from me.

The great news is this: into the darkness of such discomfiting admission shines the brilliant truth that my Lord and Savior, in His absolute commitment to me, has blocked my path. He has walled me in to prevent my most self-destructive tendencies. He has faithfully pulled me from doom's brink so I can say, with Israel, "I will go back to my husband as at first, for then I was better off than now" (Hosea 2:7b).

Prayer: O Lord, I cannot begin to fathom the depths of Your love for me, passion that loves even as it disciplines. Thank You for multiplied mercies.

Consider:

In what, other than in God, have you sought satisfaction?

_____

_____

What has been the result? _____

_____

_____

Are you still doing it? _____

_____

Have you confessed it to anyone who could hold you accountable for change? _____

Day 21

Idols At Risk

Yet all of this does not satisfy me every time I see
Mordecai the Jew sitting at the king's gate.
Esther 5:13

Observation: Haman had been elevated to high position by the king. From his lofty role, he arrogantly demanded that all the king's subjects bow before him and pay him homage. As a faithful Jew, Mordecai could not give such honor. Nor, Haman realized, could any other Jew who was captive in the land. In frustration, Haman called his wife and friends together to express his anger. He had been appointed to great honor and given glorious riches; he even had such supposed favor from Queen Esther that he alone had been invited to join the king as Esther's private banquet guest. But in spite of these honors, Haman could still say, "Yet all of this does not satisfy me every time I see Mordecai sitting at the gate."

Application: Poor, stupid Haman. He is walking into a trap that will prove his ultimate destruction. The bait is his own heart's intoxication with the false authority of worldly riches and power bestowed by earthly honor. His doom is further assured by gathering his wife and closest friends as an audience for his vindictive rants. From such as these there could be nothing but worldly advice, for they were but sycophants, groupies who no doubt enhanced their own social standing by their proximity to Haman's power.

It is easy to imagine that Haman and his friends would descend that evening into a pool of morose self-pity from which an evil plan would emerge. Mordecai should be hanged even as the wider plot was to destroy all Jews.

Could I imagine myself ever behaving as Haman? Sadly, yes. My own false pride holds the capacity for deep wounding. Such wounding leads to self-justifying scheming to regain or expand my rights—rights to which Christ has called me to die. In jealously defending my rights, I would, of course, never seek Godly counsel; my condition in that moment is not such to receive it. Instead, I gather other wounded, and we tickle one another's ears with stories of mutual offense.

These are idols all, false idols leading to destruction. What was it God had said? "You shall have no other gods before Me" (Ex. 20:3). In my area of greatest internal tension today can I honestly say I have no idols at risk? Isn't my distress caused by clinging tightly to them?

Prayer: Lord Jesus, You see my heart. You know what motivates me in those seasons when I permit other gods to hold sway. Break my heart over Your truth, Lord, that I might not be crushed by Your judgments. Yours is the kingdom, and the glory, and the power, forever.

Consider:

When have you struck out at someone, either directly or through gossip, over a violation of your supposed rights? _____
_____
_____
_____

What resulted? _____
_____
_____

What did you learn? _____
_____
_____

Day 22

FROM OOZE TO YOU

You created all things and by your will they
were created and have their being.
REVLATION 4:11 (NIV)

Observation: This passage was written by John after God invited
him to "come up here" (v. 1) to see heaven's throne room. John
reported seeing someone sitting on the throne surrounded by
dazzling colors, blazing lamps, and twenty-four other thrones,
each seating an elder. The scene was accompanied by lightning
flashes, rumblings, and peals of thunder. As the elders worshipped,
they repeatedly fell before God and laid their crowns before the
throne saying, "You are worthy our Lord and God, to receive glory
and honor and power, for you created all things and by your will
they were created and have their being" (vv. 10–11).

Application: Look closely at what the elders are saying: God is
worthy to receive glory, honor, and power because, why? Because
He created all things. Literally everything we can see or imagine
exists because God was its creator.

This is heaven's song, the song that will be sung for all eternity
before the throne of God. Verse 8 describes four living creatures
around the throne who day and night never stop saying, "Holy,
holy, holy is the Lord God Almighty who was, and is, and is to
come." It is the never-ending testimony of these creatures to which
the elders respond by praising God who merits adoration precisely
because He is the creator of, literally, every thing.

If it is God's creation (and therefore His ownership) of everything
that stimulates eternal worship of Him, is it any wonder that the
God of this age would focus with such severity on opposing that

message? For all of recorded history since Genesis 1, men have acknowledged God as creator. Yet as the end of the age draws near, Satan has advanced the deception that I and everything I see are the product of mere chance, of random evolutionary processes, thus undermining the core notion of God that heaven holds preeminent. What's the saying? "From ooze to you by way of the zoo."

If I believe that, it naturally follows that the things I in turn create are mine alone. I owe God no particular gratitude for my daily bread; I have earned it myself. The business I have built, the toys in my garage, the lake house—these are appropriate rewards for my hard work and keen perception of how to get ahead.

If He is truly the creator of all, none of this is mine: not treasure, not time, not life itself. How should that truth impact my decisions today?

Prayer: Father, You have indeed created all things. One day soon I will return to You, redeemed by Jesus' blood. Cause me to live today as though it could happen in the next insta

Consider:

Whom do you view as the owner of all you have? God, or you?

_____

_____

_____

How have you reacted when you experienced its loss? _____

_____

_____

_____

Day 23

BUYER'S REMORSE

Amaziah asked the man of God, "But what
about the hundred talents I paid for
those Israelite troops?"
2 CHRONICLES 25:9 (NIV)

Observation: Amaziah, king of Judah, was preparing to war against Edom. To augment his army he hired a hundred thousand fighting men from Israel for a hundred talents of silver (2 Chron. 25:6). After doing this he was challenged by a man of God who reminded Amaziah that the Lord was not with Israel; in fact, such alliance reflected lack of trust in God. Amaziah was told to terminate the arrangement if he wanted to experience God's blessing. Amaziah's immediate concern was for the money he had already paid to hire Israel's army, but the man of God assured him that "the LORD can give you much more than that" (v. 9).

Application: There is always a cost in following the Lord. While the benefits are eternal and wonderful beyond imagining, they are generally deferred benefits, while obedience's cost is often immediate. This was Amaziah's conundrum.

He had just paid a great deal of money to rent a shiny new army, and then came a man of God to tell him he had erred. If he used that army, God would wreak havoc on his plans. Amaziah's immediate thoughts were of buyer's remorse. He didn't express gratitude to God for heading his sin off at the pass. He wasn't thrilled by the supernatural evidence of God's watchcare. Instead, he complained about the payment he had made and what obedience would cost. Never mind that his rent-an-army agreement with Israel had been made without consulting God in the first place.

How easy it is for me to act as Amaziah acted: to make commitments for purchase of things I don't need and for which I have not consulted God. In this I am too often guilty of Paul's description of lawlessness in the last days: "People will be lovers of themselves, lovers of money, . . . without self-control, . . . rash, . . . lovers of pleasure rather than lovers of God—having a form of godliness but denying its power (2 Tim. 3:2–5).

The pleasures of comfort, like pleasures of sin, are fleeting at best. Just as there was a man of God sent to speak warning into Amaziah's life about the approaching consequences of his presumption, so God today speaks through the Holy Spirit to similarly bring correction and warning to me. The surpassingly good news is this: "The Lord can bring (me) much more than that." Immeasurable blessings are mine, heaped up and overflowing, if I will but seek Him with my whole heart and then obey.

Prayer: Lord Jesus, the passing pleasures of sin and self reliance are as nothing compared to the rewards of loving You above all else. Stir me to zealous obedience.

Consider:

Write down a time when you heard and heeded God's warning not to pursue something you badly wanted. _____

_____

_____

In obeying, how did your heart feel? _____

_____

_____

In an instance when you disobeyed, was obedience harder the next time? _____

_____

_____

Day 24

COUNTRY BOYS' BLING

I tell you the truth, not one stone here will be left
on another; every one will
be thrown down.
MATTHEW 24:2 (NIV)

Observation: Four verses earlier Jesus had mourned over Jerusalem's coming destruction, saying He had longed to protect her "as a hen gathers her chicks under her wings" (Matt. 23:37). Then He had said, "Look, your house is left to you desolate" (v. 38). As if to punctuate the point He then left the temple for the last time, leaving it desolate indeed.

Application: Could anything be more desolate than the thing Christ has left? Hosea 9:12 says, "Woe to them indeed when I depart," and depart He had.

The disciples, naturally, still didn't get it. Like me, they still too often viewed things through fleshly prisms. They were impressed by the beauty of the building itself (Matt. 24:1), and it was indeed magnificent, built with gleaming white stones and adorned with artwork and fancy bling unequalled anywhere. Like country boys come to the big city, the disciples' focus was outward. Jesus, though, never valued external edifices. When He wept, it was for lost souls. His grieving was always for the human heart bereft of relationship with its creator. The temple structure, sumptuous as it was, had been sullied by prostitutes and money changers; it held no attraction for Him.

As if to emphasize the point, He said that every stone would be thrown down. He wasn't foretelling the temple's eventual rot; the passing centuries would not merely cause decay; that would be far too passive an end. No, this particular building had a laser-guided weapon aimed at its heart. He had in mind a proactive, aggressive, intentional destruction, one that would be accomplished by God Himself, just as it would be God who three days later would grasp the thick temple veil in His mighty hands and rip it from top to bottom.

With God's language being crystal clear, why am I so like the disciples, enamored of outward things? Why do flashy cars and big houses capture my attention? More to the point, why do I hope others might be similarly impressed with my holdings? I must confess how easily captured I am by such foolishness. Like a child building a high tower with blocks, all will come crashing down when the younger sibling approaches to purposely smash it. The issue isn't simply that those things won't survive into eternity, but that God hates my focus on them even now. Seeing my wrong priorities, He promises to intentionally throw all those things down till nothing remains save my utter reliance upon Him.

Prayer: Lord Jesus, in Your pursuit of a voluntary lover You find it necessary to lay siege to every system, every thing, that I have lifted above You. The very thought of that takes my breath away, yet I want more than anything to cooperate with You. Make me like You, Lord.

Consider:

What do you try to do to balance pursuit of God with pursuit of worldly pleasures? _____

_____

_____

How has it worked out? _____

_____

What does God require differently of you? _____

_____

_____

Day 25

MILKWEED AND COCKLEBURS

He asked them, "Why have you been standing
here all day long doing nothing?
MATTHEW 20:6 (NIV)

Observation: Jesus's question comes early in the parable of workers in the vineyard. The landowner had hired workmen early in the day for a fair wage. Then, apparently needing more workers, he had gone again at the third, sixth, ninth, and eleventh hours to hire still more at the same daily rate promised the original hires. His payment of identical wages for very dissimilar labor tested the hearts of those hired first.

Application: The story is a familiar one, and its ending point an important test of both my heart and that of the Jews who had been originally chosen by God. Yet I am captured by the question, "Why have you been standing here all day doing nothing?" In verse 3 Jesus said the landowner "saw others standing in the marketplace doing nothing." Again in verse 6 he "found still others standing around."

Why this seemingly critical evaluation of how the unemployed were described? The report could as well have read that the men were in the marketplace seeking work, but instead there is a decidedly pointed tilt toward emphasizing their shiftlessness. The Lord's criticism of this posture speaks clearly of His evaluation of how they were spending their time. In the next chapter comes reinforcement of the same theme, this time applied to an unproductive fig tree. Jesus's hunger caused Him to approach a fig tree only to find it barren of fruit, so He addressed the tree, "May you never bear fruit again!" Immediately the tree withered (Matth. 21:18–19).

From all this it seems clear that I ought to be productively engaged. After all, was I not created to work? Didn't God intend from the beginning that I work in the garden? Ummm, no, that was a trick question. Such fleshly reasoning can creep in to steer me away from God's best.

I was created for fellowship with God, not to pull weeds in an already perfect garden. I was created for intimacy. His design of me was that I would press in to know Him, to love Him, to enjoy His presence. At the end of the day it isn't His evaluation of my straight-as-an-arrow furrows that will bless Him, nor His survey of land kept free of milkweed and cockleburs. His evaluation of me will turn on one thing only: like the fig tree, has my life produced what He intended, or have I spent my days laboring in sweaty pursuit of lesser ends? Have I pressed into relationship with Him, or settled for the world's affirmation of my success?

Prayer: Lord Jesus, I don't want Your evaluation of me to ever be that I was standing around doing nothing. No matter the work of my hands, help me to keep my mind, will, and emotions fully focused upon You.

Consider:

What has God been speaking to your heart about regarding how you spend your time? _____

_____

_____

_____

What has been the fruit of your response? _____

_____

_____

Who will you ask to hold you accountable for change in this area?

_____

When will you ask them? _____

Day 26

THE DEEP

In the beginning, God created the heavens and the
earth. Now the earth was formless and empty,
darkness was over the surface of the deep…
GENESIS 1:1–2

Observation: Time now begins. The uncreated, eternal God who
had till now communed within Himself as Father, Son, and Holy
Spirit, created. No light yet existed for there was nothing to be
observed except an unwieldy, heavy, swirling mass of material
where none had existed a moment before. Untamed waters mixed
with amorphous elements to form chaos—an unimaginably huge
mixture from which God would later form the heavens and the
firmament called earth.

Application: Darkness was profound, not because God created the
darkness, but because He had not yet created light. The formless
chaos was said to be empty, yet it had a surface to it, a surface which
covered what could only be called "the deep."

Thinking about this, the senses are helpless; they require a refer-
ence point or they are reduced to meaninglessness. To understand what this "deep" must have been like, two ideas come to
mind. First is the grave . . . not the grave as experenced by
mourners seated on bright green astro-turf at its yawing entry,
but the grave as experienced by one who inhabits it forever with
no hope of eternal life in Christ's glorious presence, sealed in a box of
steel, sunk into a concrete sarcophagus, covered by tons of dirt.

The second idea for understanding the deep is related to
the first. It is both the pre-grave and the post-grave darkness
inhabited forever by the soul never infused with the light and life
of Christ. Jeremiah 4:23 speaks to the power of unregenerate
sin to recreate this darkness when he says, "I looked at the

earth and it was formless and empty, and at the heavens, and their light was gone."

I was born into a sin-darkened world. Until I reunited with my Creator God through the redemption of His Son, my life could never overcome the morass of deep darkness that overwhelmed my soul. The conviction for me in this is how casually I consider the utter darkness of the lost. Having been delivered unto the light so many years ago, I no longer spend much time contemplating the deep's darkness, yet I should. Such thought will radically impact what I do with money, with relationships, and with every moment of time I have left on this earth. In a moment, I will move back into the glorious light of timeless eternity. But what about her? What about him?

Prayer: Father, it seems odd to think about heavy, unending darkness as part of my devotional time this morning, yet it is a profound reminder that my salvation wasn't just for me. Others, too, desperately need to find rescue as I did. Move upon my heart, Lord, even as you moved upon the deep.

***

Consider:

Do you give generously of time and money to win the lost to Christ?

It is not unreasonable for financial loss to result in a cutback in our giving. But sometimes the cutback is greater than necessary; other times we cut back in fear of possible loss. How have you done this?

Why?

Day 27

SEEING PAST THE SMOKE

Moreover, your little ones who you said would
become a prey, and your sons, who this day have no
knowledge of good or evil, shall enter there, and
I will give it to them and they shall possess it.

DEUTERONOMY 1:39

Observation: The early chapters of Deuteronomy describe the Israelites poised at the edge of the Promised Land. They were finally ready to enter after forty years of wandering in the desert as the nation waited for the rebellious generation of adults to die off or to be killed by God (see Deut. 2:15). In today's reading, God was reminding the people that one of the foolish justifications their parents had used for their disobedience to God was "concern" for the safety of their children.

God's response nearly forty years later is that not only will those little ones be kept safe by Him, but in fact, they are the very ones who will have the privilege of crossing over into the land God had first made available to their parents two generations earlier.

Application: It is painful to remember so many times in the past when I have tried to justify disobedience to what I knew God was saying with the claim that it was "for the benefit of my family," or even more stupidly, "to serve the Lord." I remember many lonely nights in motel rooms as I traveled the nation when our children were young. My speaking and working supposedly was to earn a living for them or to help the needy of the world. The reality was that the Holy Spirit was wooing me to treat as higher priority my family's need for my daily presence.

I suspect I am not alone in living by such an ill-advised priority system. Though I may blow smoke about how "I'm doing this for you, for us," God sees through my real motives perfectly.

Finally, through my wife, Cindy's, illness God got my attention and wrung out of me the need to succeed in the world's eyes by making a radical change in my lifestyle. He taught me that nothing is more important than obedience to Him in even the smallest detail.

Prayer: Father, I pray that these lessons, once learned, will not have to be repeated. Forgive me, Lord, for each action I have taken to pursue notoriety or fame or impact beyond the field You have provided for me to labor in.

Consider:

How have your priorities changed of late, such as the way you spend your time and money? _____

_____

_____

_____

_____

What further changes has God been speaking to you about?

_____

_____

_____

_____

What other person have you shared this with? _____

_____

_____

Day 28

LIVING WITH PRICKS AND THORNS

You shall drive out all the inhabitants of the land
from before you, and destroy all their figured
stones, and destroy all their molten images
and demolish all their high places; and you shall
take possession of the land and live in it, for
I have given the land to you to possess it. . . . But if
you do not drive out the inhabitants of
the land from before you, then it shall come about
that those whom you let remain of them
will become as pricks in your eyes and as thorns
in your sides, and they shall trouble you
in the land in which you live.
NUMBERS 33:52–53, 55

Observation: These verses perfectly foreshadow and encompass the Gospel message. The Israelites had entered the Promised Land, and God told them to drive out all the old inhabitants, to sweep the land completely clean of every old idol, every thing and every place that had once been an object or a place of worship. It was to be warfare of the kind that would take no prisoners, to brook no compromises. The consequences of disobedience in this weren't that they were going to be thrown out of the land to wander in the wilderness again. No, they were going to have constant trouble, constant irritation, and a lack of peace.

Application: Living in freedom is a choice, not a guarantee. The Israelites were told to enter into the land, and they had done so. But their possession of it had to be complete.

The relationship of this passage to the Gospel message is this: simply accepting Christ as Savior is merely the beginning step, equivalent to the Israelites' entering into the land. But then I must do the hard work of dispossessing every old idol, every old habit, every enemy and all their possessions. If I don't, I will be a miserable Christian indeed, living not in victory, but with the pricks and thorns that have every right to afflict me because I have not turned them out completely.

I want Christ to bless and "clean up" my old life, but He wants to bring everything about my old self to utter and complete death. Every remnant of my old flesh life is to be crucified with Christ so He is free to begin writing a new story on my heart.

Prayer: Father, You are a jealous God. You say I am to have "no other gods" but You. Show me, Lord, every area of my life where I am clinging to something You want me to surrender—whether it be relationships that aren't life-giving or possessions I hang on to out of financial fears or habits that weren't formed under Your watchful gaze. All these things, Lord, I choose to put to death so I can enter into true life in You.

Consider:

Compared to an earlier season in your life, what are the evidences that you are living in freedom today? _____
_____
_____
_____
_____

What, if any, bondage do you sense may still be residing within?
_____
_____
_____

Who else knows about this? _____

If no one. when will you tell someone? _____

Day 29

Stones Must Fall

And Jesus said to him, "Do you see these great
buildings? Not one stone shall be
left upon another which will not be torn down."
Mark 13:2

Observation: A student of Jesus had just remarked on the beauty and magnificence of the surrounding buildings as they came out of the temple. As delighted by the works of men's hands as the student was, Jesus struck to the heart of pride. He pierced through any satisfaction in temporal accomplishment by saying that it all had to come down.

Application: Was there anywhere a construction project more magnificent than the Jerusalem temple? Had not Solomon brought together the finest artisans and carpenters, and gathered the most precious building materials, to make this house for God? Hadn't God's own presence been manifest there?

We do the same thing today, spending months with architects and boards of directors, lining up lenders and meeting with governing authorities seeking permits for various aspects of our construction projects. We raise up mighty corporations and spend the bulk of our lives primarily in relationship with colleagues, not with family. We push to pay off the mortgage between the time the kids are out of college and the date of our retirement, working feverishly at the same time to build up an impressive 401(k). How much like my own heart are those buildings that looked so good to the outward observer. But Jesus said that all stones must fall.

He knows that my heart can be hard and cold as stones at times, prideful over accomplishments or possessions. But His purpose is to break my heart, to utterly defeat pride of accomplishment, to tear down every high thing I have lifted up in my own strength and in my own eyes.

Prayer: Lord Jesus, thank You that You are teaching me to cooperate with the work You want to do in and through me. I'm sorry for being such a slow learner, and I repent and ask Your forgiveness for every instance of stubbornness or rebellion against the correcting things You have wanted to do in my life. I want my life, my family, to be something You have built, Lord—something that will stand for all eternity. Show me day by day what my part is in the work You are doing in my own heart. Thank You, Lord.

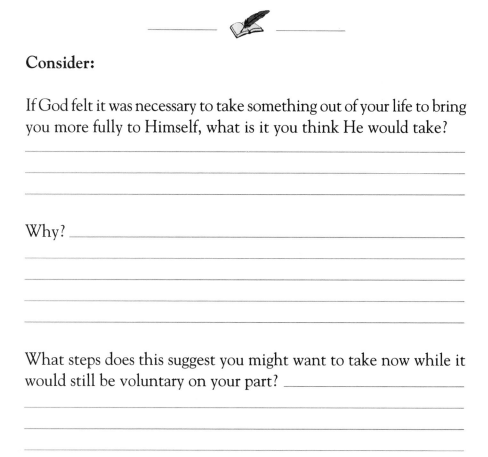

Consider:

If God felt it was necessary to take something out of your life to bring you more fully to Himself, what is it you think He would take?

_____

_____

_____

Why? _____

_____

_____

_____

What steps does this suggest you might want to take now while it would still be voluntary on your part? _____

_____

_____

Day 30

ENTERING THE LAND

So Joshua said to the sons of Israel, "How long will
you put off entering to take possession of
the land which the LORD, the God of
your fathers, has given you?"

JOSHUA 18:3

Observation: All Israel had assembled following the conquering of the land, but seven tribes had not yet divided and claimed their inheritance. So Joshua devised a plan for having tribal representatives reach agreement as to what portion each tribe should take.

Application: The cry of Joshua to the Israelites is the same as the cry of God's heart to His people today: "How long will you put off entering to take possession of the land which the Lord has given you?" Some among us have heard the Gospel and know intellectually what God purchased on the Cross, but still fail to walk in it. Others have been baptized in the past; still others have confessed Christ as Savior at some point, but have never fully laid hold of the reality of a changed life.

How the cry of God's heart for us today is reflected in Joshua's words!

My heart is heavy with thoughts of so many friends and family members who are in similar situations described above. They have heard but not responded. They know what Christ has done but have turned away or put off their response. Because of that, so many will go into eternity in their lost condition.

Then I examine the ways in which I fall short of "taking possession of all the land which the Lord has given" me, and I am undone by what I see. My personal priorities leave no room for thinking critically of others; instead, I must fall on my face in repentance for pursuing an inheritance of my own design rather than laying claim to His riches.

Prayer: Lord, You have offered me such a wonderful, wide expanse of rich land, so much opportunity to impact the world for Christ, and yet I fall so far short. Teach me day by day what it is to be truly responsive to You, not just to have a glad heart about all You have done for me. Help me turn that gladness into a good use of time and resources so land purchased by Your blood will bear much fruit.

Consider:

In what ways have you tried to design your own path to God?

How has it worked?

What needs to change?

Day 31

JUST STUFF

He brought out his people with rejoicing,
his chosen ones with shouts of joy; he gave them the
lands of the nations, and they fell heir
to what others had toiled for...
PSALM 105:43–44 (NIV)

Observation: Psalm 105 is a remarkable record of God's fulfillment of His covenant with Abraham. It is a clarion call to praise and worship in recognition of God's faithfulness to Israel from their earliest history. He reminds them of the famine in Canaan and His preparation of Joseph to be their deliverer as Egypt's prime minister. He recounts the signs and wonders performed through Moses and Aaron to deliver them out of Egypt, and speaks of His watchcare during their years in the desert. The chapter closes as it began, with a reminder of His covenant with Abraham (v. 42) which He says He remembers forever (v. 8). As a result, God says He gave them the lands of the nations, and they fell heir to what others had toiled for.

Application: This psalm is like a love letter tenderly written by a father who wants his children to remember their family heritage. We all long to know our roots, to have some sense of the characters and events that formed us. "What were their struggles, their victories?" we wonder. "What sort of demons did they have to face down for me to be here today?" We give our parents blank legacy books and hope they would fill them with remembrances that might paint a fuller picture of the family's heritage.

Psalm 105 is God's legacy letter. He focuses primarily on His divine initiatives rather than on the people's shortcomings, and He closes by pointing out that they fell heir to what others had toiled for.

Think about the implications of that statement. There are some who toil and some who reap. Some spend backbreaking lives working in their own strength to build their kingdom upon the earth, only to see it slip through their fingers in the end as God rewards those who have "kept His precepts and observed His laws" (v. 45). How futile are my best efforts outside the will of God. He says that in the end, the fruit of such toil will bless others. In this we glimpse the truth of Proverbs 13:22, "a sinner's wealth is stored up for the righteous."

Just as for Israel, God has had a plan for me from the beginning. I, too, have a promised land where His reward awaits. It is my choice to end my personal desert wanderings, pursuing rewards I hope to create for myself. Ultimately, my desire is to be God's heir; only in His inheritance will I find "rest from [my] enemies . . . and live in safety" (Deut. 12:10). Everything else is just "stuff."

Prayer: Lord, You have promised an inheritance that can never perish, spoil, or fade. Bring my heart into alignment with Yours. I don't want to waste another minute pursuing less than Your best.

Consider:

How have your own desert wanderings delayed fulfillment of God's destiny for you? _____

_____

_____

What do you need to lay down in order to enter into all He has for you?

_____

_____

Who have you asked to help you with accountability in this area? _____

_____

Day 32

SAND CASTLES

Even wise men die; the stupid and senseless alike
perish and leave their wealth to others. Their
inner thought is that their houses are forever and
their dwelling places to all generations. They
have called their lands after their own names, but
man in his pomp will not endure; he is
like the beasts that perish.
PSALM 49:10–12

Observation: This passage speaks of the utter foolishness of men trying to make their mark on the world by working on goals or projects or priorities that were not set for them by God. Everything else, no matter how diligently we pursue excellence and success, will be destroyed in the fires of a God who burns up all works of man's devising. The only lasting mark we can make is when we do His work in His way. Everything else is rubble.

Application: My perspective is profoundly more limited than God's, so I have little ability to anticipate all the ways in which my labors may be reduced to rubble. I am like the child who, never having experienced the force of the tides, is building a sand castle at seashore. There is an inexorable power heading toward my diligent efforts that will utterly wipe away any trace of my having labored in the sands, but I am oblivious to it.

In the same way, God is saying that all the things I put my hand to are like that childish sand castle.

It is so easy to look back on my life and shamefully realize the many things I have done that God wasn't in. The more frightening thing is to examine all the things to which I currently give my life, my time, my money. How much of my current efforts are more kingdom-oriented than those of the past?

To make eternal impact requires constant reevaluation, constant pleas for the Lord to make His view known, and unrelenting willingness on my part to agree with God's view of things.

Prayer: Lord, I pray that You would find me spending my life more wisely today than was the case yesterday, and that tomorrow I'll be more effective still. Cause me to be clear-eyed and of good hearing as You evaluate the commitments of my life, for I know that my story is only written in this life, moment by moment. When the wrath of Your judgment is released, when Your glance of fiery righteousness falls upon the work of my hands at the end of this life, I pray that You will be pleased. Show me how to walk that narrow road day by day.

Consider:

What are the names of your three favorite sandcastles?
1. _____
2. _____
3. _____

How do you know they are sandcastles? _____
_____
_____
_____
_____

How satisfying is your pursuit of them? _____
_____
_____
_____

Day 33

RECEIVING A DOUBLE PORTION

But to Hannah he would give a double
portion, for he loved Hannah, but the LORD
had closed her womb.

1 SAMUEL 1:5

Observation: Though Hannah was much loved by her husband, she was barren. Her husband's response, because of his deep love, was not critical of her. He did not heap further condemnation on her. Rather, he gave even more of himself to her—a "double portion."

Application: How like the Lord, who says to the poor and downtrodden and meek of the earth that He will bless them. In fact, the meek are to inherit the earth (see Matt. 5:5, NIV), which shows intent of physical blessing now as well as the spiritual blessing that comes to all who accept His gift of eternal life through Jesus Christ.

Hannah's story is a wonderful picture of God's love for the afflicted of the earth. But it also conveys a hard-to-accept truth about the afflicted. It says that God Himself had closed her womb. We should pay special attention to that. He blesses whom He will, often in ways and for purposes we cannot imagine. God had a special calling planned for the son she would one day bear, although she could not know that at the time. Instead, she was "greatly distressed" and "wept bitterly" (1 Sam. 1:10).

Today, it's very easy to live with little personal contact with the poor of the earth. When God places poor people in our midst, do we respond like Hannah's husband, heaping a double portion on them?

Prayer: Lord, sensitize my heart to the poor of the earth, and to the poor in our midst. Cause my heart to be softened, that I might approach them with a heart of compassion. Let me have Your heart for the poor, that it might affect how I spend the time and money You have allotted to me.

Consider:

How are you investing in the poor of the earth? _____

_____

_____

_____

_____

_____

What else is God speaking to you about doing? _____

_____

_____

_____

_____

_____

What more do you require to obey? _____

_____

_____

_____

_____

_____

Day 34

GRACE FOR FULLNESS

And everyone who has left houses or brothers or
sisters or father or mother or children or farms
for My name's sake, will receive many times as
much, and will inherit eternal life. But many who
are first will be last; and the last, first.
MATTHEW 19:29–30

Observation: Jesus in this sweeping passage summed up what is required to enter into His eternal life.

Application: Jesus calls me to turn to Him wholeheartedly, hanging on to nothing of the past—none of the old relationships and systems of self-identity.

As one example of how to leave everything yet not forsake the very Law that Christ came to fulfill, consider the matter of finances. The Israelites were commanded to give not one tithe, but three. They further were commanded to tithe their capital every seventh year, and every forty-nine years they were to cancel all debts. The Pharisees were noted for their very public way of calculating their tithe, even carefully counting mustard seeds. There was in their heart none of the lavish joy the Lord wanted to see in them. They held no wonder in recognizing that all they had was a gift from God, a gift to hold loosely and give freely and eagerly.

Some today want to use Paul's words that we are "no longer under the law" (Rom. 6:14) to live a life free from the disciplines required for us to be fully yoked to Christ. A yoke is a firm, inflexible thing, and my flesh resists it. Yet if I want to be fully His, then His yoke is required, but Jesus said His yoke is easy (Matt. 11:30).

Others may simply have not carefully considered the nature of the Word of God. The Bible is one book not two. Jesus and

His original disciples were Jewish to the core; the only writings they had were the Old Testament—what they called the Law and the Prophets. When Jesus quoted Scripture, it was the Old Testament. Paul and a few other disciples completed God's book of guidance for His people through letters recording exploits of the early believers.

God repeatedly calls me to things that are hard, that go against my human nature. He says He came to fulfill the law and recognizes that apart from Him I will fall short.

Prayer: Lord, all I know to do is, like Paul, to "press on toward the goal for the prize of the upward call of God in Christ Jesus" (Phil. 3:14). Thank You for Your grace when I fail. Thank You for covering my sin and my shortcomings, and continually coaxing me to walk in more of Your fullness. Give me a generous heart, Lord, to daily become more like you by responding to Your grace and mercy.

Consider:

What is the hardest thing God is calling you to? _____
_____
_____

What makes it hard? _____
_____
_____

What would have to change for you to say yes to God? _____
_____
_____

Who is praying with you about this? _____

If no one, when will you recruit a prayer partner? _____

Day 35

WHEELBARROWS AND TANKERS

So she went from him and shut the door behind her and
her sons; they were bringing the vessels to her and
she poured. When the vessels were full, she said to her
son, "Bring me another vessel." And he said to
her, "There is not one vessel more." And the oil stopped.

2 KINGS 4:5–6

Observation: This widow's sons were about to be taken from her by creditors who were pressing legitimate claims following the death of her husband. Elisha had told her to borrow vessels from her neighbors, and to then begin pouring into them her small supply of oil. As she began pouring, what little oil she had became much. Her small treasure of oil filled every vessel she had borrowed, and then the oil stopped.

Application: At least two kingdom principles are illustrated in this story. First, she had enough faith for basic obedience; she indeed borrowed vessels and she began pouring. But one wonders why she had not borrowed more vessels? Did she come to regret having "some" faith, enough to borrow just "some" vessels, but not having enough faith to borrow all the jars and wheelbarrows and tankers in the county? How did the limits of her faith limit the extent of God's miracle in her behalf?

Second, this incident is also a wonderful reminder that God creates out of nothing. I tend to look at my need—more income to pay the bills, or larger-than-ever pledges to build a church— and I can't imagine the need being met precisely because in my humanness I believe that a generous supply always costs me more. If I want more income, I must work harder or longer or smarter. If I want to give more generously, it's going to be at the expense of my retirement security or some other thing I have been saving for.

But His provision is never met at my expense; it does not depend upon my efforts. After all, I am supposed to have already surrendered everything to Him. When He supplies, there is always more than before. I should remember this when my needs loom large, whether needs for my daily life or my desire to respond when God calls me to be "impossibly" generous. When He supplies He goes far and above what I could have imagined. If it were otherwise, it would not have been a miracle, and God's hand would not have been required. Do I really want to respond just out of my own strength and resources or out of God's?

PRAYER: Father God, You who created out of nothing all I can see or imagine, I want to live in a way that increases my reliance upon You. Convict me of wrong when my human calculus is about to limit my response to what You have called me to do. O creator God, pour Your abundance before me. The work is Yours. The effort is Yours. To You be the glory!

Consider:

Think of a time when God proved to you that obeying Him gave you benefits even greater than the cost. _____

_____

_____

What is He asking of you now that you are still fearful about agreeing to? _____

_____

_____

Day 36

TRAIN WRECK

Israel is a luxuriant vine; he produces fruit for himself.
The more his fruit, the more altars he made.

HOSEA 10:1

Observation: The context of Hosea 10:1 is that as the people became more prosperous, they had less need to rely upon God and began to build their own altars. This is an echo of Hosea 8:11, which speaks of having built "multiplied altars" that became places of sinning. The rest of the chapter describes God's response: He would destroy literally everything the people had come to value other than God Himself.

Application: This verse is a spiritual mirror if ever one existed. Altars: 401k plans, IRAs, houses, careers, ministries. I see my own reflection, filled from earliest days with a stubborn determination to be independent, to "make it" on my own, to do well.

But who is to say what "doing well" looks like? Have I asked God's opinion lately? Or dare I not, for fear His opinion could mean total derailment and train wreck from tracks so feverishly laid down? The Gospel of Christ is a downward call insofar as this life is concerned. It is a call I strain against, a call to simplicity of lifestyle and singularity of focus. A call away from entitlement. It's terrifying, because the more I understand it, the more I realize it is the complete opposite of the mentality I have learned to live by.

In my prosperity, I do indeed build my own altars. I worship at them, asking God to bless my plans and the work of my hands. The possibility that these plans, these works, may not be His plan and works is too profoundly troubling for me to seriously consider. But verse 12 tells how to right things: "Sow with a view to righteousness, reap in accordance with kindness; break up your fallow ground, for it is time to seek the LORD until He comes to rain righteousness on you." And again in Psalm 73:25–26, "Besides You, I desire nothing on earth. My flesh and my heart may fail, but God is the strength of my heart and my portion forever."

PRAYER: O God, You Who have made all that my eyes delight in, You are indeed all I need. Pull me back today, Lord, from the precipice of my own pursuits, and cause my heart to exalt You and You alone. Teach me contentment in less, Lord, for as I make You my only refuge, You open storehouses of heaven as my portion in You. Rain Your righteousness on me today, Lord. I love You!

Consider:

If you were to take Hosea 10:12 seriously (i.e., sowing with a view toward righteousness, reaping in accordance with kindness) what might change in your day-to-day life? _____

_____

_____

_____

_____

How have you applied the idea of there being a "downward call" of Christ on your life? _____

_____

_____

_____

_____

Day 37

COOKIE-JAR GIVING

On the first day of every week, each one of you
should set aside a sum of money
in keeping with his income, saving it up
so when I come no collection
will have to be made.
1 CORINTHIANS 16:2 (NIV)

Observation: Paul's request was consistent with what he also asked of the church at Galatia (see 1 Cor. 16:1). They should commit to a regular, sustained practice of setting aside money to advance the spread of the Gospel. He didn't want to leave the financial health of the expanding Christian movement to the occasional special offering; nor did he want believers to miss an opportunity for generosity. Instead, he envisioned that each believer would embrace the personal responsibility of setting aside money to be given when Paul came to town.

Application: Now Paul really began meddling. He went far beyond reminding those early Christians of their responsibility to tithe. He even exceeded usual admonitions to give generously and cheerfully. Occasional special giving, offerings gathered after a missionary's particularly compelling report, are not enough. We are all familiar with these appeals: a dear saint arrives armed with PowerPoint and compelling tales of spiritual battles fought and won in darkest Africa or deep in the Amazon's damp recesses. To gin up a generous response, we are told that our offering ought to be generous, given joyfully beyond what we had in mind when the service began.

Such causes are often appropriate, and a generous impulse within the redeemed heart always is. But Paul here calls us to something beyond a heart-felt response to a good cause. He calls us instead to a lifestyle of living below our means. He challenges me to make daily choices in spending so I might regularly accumulate a fund for lavishing into the kingdom when those special opportunities arise. In this, my giving would be not merely from what's in my wallet that morning, but rather from what's in the cookie jar at home. Gradually, I begin to understand that such generosity can only come from moderating my lifestyle, reducing debt, becoming content with personal consumption of smaller servings of the good life.

Recreation, clothing, and travel; toys, entertainment, and housing, the day-by-day decisions I make profoundly impact my ability to live as Paul asked. I must ask myself, Does Christ's claim to my heart truly include what I earn? Have I adjusted my personal priorities with eternity in view? Neither adherence to the principles of tithing nor my impulse to empty that day's purse at hearing the next good appeal are adequate responses to what Christ has done for me.

Prayer: Lord Jesus, You have led me to make many decisions to live beneath my means for the greater good of Your kingdom, but I yet have far to go. Speak to me in each remaining area, Lord; help me to further simplify my lifestyle in light of Your claim on my life.

Consider:

In what ways have you chosen to live beneath your means? _____
_____
_____

When was the last time your generosity surprised even you? _____
_____
_____
_____

What were the aftereffects? _____
_____

Day 38

HOGWASH

You shall not delay the offering from your
harvest and your vintage. The firstborn of your
sons you shall give to Me. You shall do the same
with your oxen and with your sheep. It shall be
with its mother seven days; on the eighth day
you shall give it to Me."
EXODUS 22:29–30

Observation: This passage comes under the heading of "laws concerning civil and religious obligations," particularly relating to how God's people were to handle their finances.

Application: God is manifestly serious about expecting me to give the first fruits of whatever I have, whether it is children, animals, crops, income or time. In this passage is the sense of command (you *shall* not delay, the firstborn of your sons you *shall* give to me, you *shall*, you *shall*). There is also the requirement of immediacy (you shall not delay).

God considers the gift of my first fruits to be holy, which doesn't seem to leave much room for negotiation. But Lord! I have been laid off and cannot pay the rent this month. But Father, my earnings are so meager I don't know how I will put food on the table. But Lord, You know how desperately we need that vacation. On and on it goes.

What is not scriptural in the slightest sense is the oft-heard encouragement to "just begin by giving what you can. If you cannot give the full tithe, then start with just two or three percent." How shall God ever be put to the test of Malachi 3:10 if I do not bring the whole tithe and all required offerings into the storehouse? How can I ever hope to rely upon God's provision if I have not thrown my needy self at His feet by obeying His commands in the matter of giving?

The kingdom doesn't work this way: "I hear you God; I know what You have said, but I will not do so this month. However, I do look forward to Your great blessings." Hogwash! He established the pattern by giving for me His only Son; how shall I excuse myself from following His model?

No excuse, no perceived lack or shortfall can be a reason for withholding my gifts to the Lord. I must do what He has already done.

Prayer: Lord, You have modeled lavish generosity in Your gift to me; cause my heart to respond by overflowing with generosity in return. Make me quick to give.

Consider:

Think of an instance when you were scrupulously obedient in giving what God required of you even though circumstances made it seem impossible. _____

_____

How did God provide? _____

_____

_____

Are you secretly withholding now something He has required of you?

_____

What is it, and why? _____

_____

_____

Day 39

JOANNA'S CROWN

Joanna the wife of Chuza, Herod's steward, and
Susanna, and many others . . . were contributing to their
support out of their private means.
LUKE 8:3

Observation: Luke 8:1–3 addresses how the ministry of Jesus was funded. Jesus and the twelve disciples were in a season of great activity, moving from one city or village to another, proclaiming and preaching the kingdom of God. Luke describes such a breadth of activity that we can only conclude it must have been exhausting. No time for tentmaking for this passionate band. Their schedule would never permit it. So, how were they supported? Who gave the funds needed for their food, warm showers, and nights in the local Motel 6?

Verse 3 mentions Joanna as being a key donor. Here is one of the delights of Scripture, as Luke lets us in on something that must have caused him to smile as he wrote. Joanna, it turns out, was the wife of Chuza whose name, except for this one passage, might otherwise have been lost to history. Chuza was Herod's steward, a man in a position of considerable importance in the management of Herod's finances. This was the same Herod who had beheaded John the Baptist (see Matt. 14; Mark 6). Ironically, the money of this evil king was being used to finance the spread of the Gospel.

Application: What a delightful thought! The wife of one of Herod's inner circle was funneling family resources to the very thing Herod had hoped to stop. Have you ever wondered why Jesus, knowing full well of Judas's thievery from the disciples' treasury, nonetheless allowed him to continue as keeper of the moneybags? Jesus knew His needs would be met, even from the treasury of the king of evil himself.

God will not be thwarted; His purposes will be accomplished. The only question I should ask is, will I get in on what He's up to? Surely Joanna's contributions came at great personal risk; if Chuza had ever reviewed her checkbook ledger, Joanna's head would certainly have rolled as John's had. Yet because she said yes to God, she will be known through all the ages as one whose life bore eternal fruit. Not because she preached. Not because she taught. Not because she raised the dead or healed anyone. She was simply someone in the background, through whose financial support Jesus did all these things and more.

Prayer: Lord Jesus, give me a generous heart. Cause me to so reorder my priorities that I can give more. Give me wisdom from on high as to how I ought to use the resources You have given me. And if You find me to be a faithful steward, pour more into the account. It is great fun to get to participate in Your work, Lord.

Consider:

Remember a time when you delighted to participate financially in something God gave you an option to do. _____
_____
_____

How did it feel to participate? _____
_____

Are you making an important difference now in the life of an individual who is spreading the Gospel? _____

If not, ask the Lord to present you with such a project or person into whose life you could make a Joanna-kind of difference. _____
_____
_____

Day 40

ORNAN'S GENEROSITY

Ornan said to David, "Take it for yourself; and let my
lord the king do what is good in his sight.
See, I will give the oxen for burnt offerings and the
threshing sledges for wood and the wheat for
a grain offering; I will give it all."
1 CHRONICLES 21:23

Observation: This one verse is all we hear of Ornan in the Scriptures, but the lessons it can teach us of lavish generosity are stunning. David had been ordered by God to build a place of worship on the site of Ornan's threshing floor, which was Ornan's place of business, his livelihood. Ornan offered to donate literally everything—the oxen that powered the equipment, the equipment itself, (sledges), and the grain, even the site itself.

Application: Here was a man not reluctant, but eager, quick, to make an incredible sacrifice. This was like a carpenter offering not only his tools, but also his workshop. I wish I knew more of Ornan, but perhaps what I learn of him from this single chapter is enough: he was a man who knew the king had a need, and was quick to offer all he had in response.

What powerful work must God have done in Ornan's life for him to be so quick to be willing to give not just from his surplus, but also from the very substance of his life! Somehow he had learned to hold these things loosely. I must conclude that Ornan was ultimately willing to trust God to take care of him. Oh, to learn that lesson myself, to get to a place where nothing I own would possess me, where literally everything would be available to use in the advance of His kingdom!

Prayer: Father, I know You have given me a desire to be a generous giver, but you ask for more than that. You call for sacrifice, which by definition should not be easy. Thank You for the joy I have known in the past and that I know now; when I give in response to what You have given, Lord, I do put my trust in You. I ask You to press in on me more, Lord, to test me and to search my heart insofar as attachment to "things" is concerned. I trust You, Lord, with my future and with my life.

Consider:

What do you own that you are possessed by? _____
_____
_____
_____

When have you, like Ornan, given everything that was needed for a particular purpose? _____
_____
_____
_____
_____

If God gave you that request now, what conditions would you put on your response? _____
_____
_____
_____

Afterword

Thank you for spending several weeks of devotional time in this book. As its author I pray you have found it to be useful in your journey with the Lord. It is His desire that you be drawn into ever-deepening intimacy with Him, and that is my prayer for you as well.

I would love to hear from you, particularly with regard to how your own journey has been impacted through these devotionals.

You may blog to me through my Web site:
www.lifeinrealtimeonline.com
or e-mail me directly at dave@lifeinrealtimeonline.com

Also on my Web site you can sign up to receive a free subscription of the daily e-mailed devotionals I write, and soon you'll be able to download daily podcasts of me reading the devotionals as well.

Finally, if you would like more such writings in a keepsake edition book, you can order 365 beautifully bound daily devotionals called *A Journey: Life In Real Time.*

Song of Songs 8:6–7 (NIV) says this: "Place me like a seal over your heart, like a seal on your arm; for love is as strong as death, its jealousy unyielding as the grave. Many waters cannot quench love; rivers cannot wash it away. If one were to give all the wealth of his house for love, it would be utterly scorned." It is my prayer that you would personally experience having Christ Himself set as a seal over your heart, and that you would experience daily the mighty flame of His unquenchable love.

Dave Keesling
Woodland Park, CO
May, 2009